Clip-Art Features for
Church Newsletters 2

Illustrations for Bulletin Boards,
Home Bulletins, and News Releases

Clip-Art Features for Church Newsletters 2

George W. Knight, Compiler
Howard Paris, Illustrator

BAKER BOOK HOUSE
Grand Rapids, Michigan 49506

Copyright 1986 by
Baker Book House Company

ISBN: 0-8010-5471-0

Third printing, June 1987

Printed in the United States of America

Contents

Introduction

Churches and religious organizations responded enthusiastically to the first compilation of *Clip-Art Features for Church Newsletters,* published by Baker Book House in 1985. So here's another collection of material in the same handy format. These copyright-free items are complete with copy, illustrations, and borders. All you have to do is clip them out and paste them down on your newsletter layout sheet for quick and easy reproduction by copying machine, electronic stencil, or offset press.

My thanks to Howard Paris of Mableton, Georgia, for the professional, eye-catching illustrations that appear in these clip-art features. His creative handiwork adds a special touch to these handy items. We hope you will find them useful in your church's publishing program.

George W. Knight

1

The Bible

I Am the Bible

I am the Bible, God's wonderful library.
I am always—and above all—the truth.
To the weary pilgrim, I am a strong staff.
To the one who sits in darkness, I am glorious light.
To those who stumble beneath heavy burdens, I am sweet rest.
To him who has lost his way, I am a safe guide.
To those who are sick in sin, I am healing strength and forgiveness.
To the discouraged, I am a glad message of hope.
To those who are distressed and tossed about by the storms of life,
I am an anchor, sure and steady.
To those who search for salvation, I reveal the Savior of the World.
I am the Bible, God's holy Word.

The Bible in a Single Verse: John 3:16

The greatest reason	For
The greatest lover	God
The greatest degree	so loved
The greatest company	the world
The greatest act	that He gave
The greatest gift	His only begotten Son
The greatest opportunity	that whosoever
The greatest simplicity	believeth
The greatest attraction	in Him
The greatest promise	should not perish
The greatest difference	but
The greatest certainty	have
The greatest possession	everlasting life.

2

The Church and Church Support

The Passing of Someone Else

The church was bowed in grief this week to learn that one of our most valuable members, Someone Else, passed away. This death creates a vacancy that will be difficult to fill. Someone Else has been with us for many years. During all these years, he did far more than a normal person's share of the work. Whenever leadership was mentioned, this wonderful person was looked to for inspiration as well as results.

Whenever there was a job to do—a class to teach, or a meeting to attend—one name was on everyone's list: "Let Someone Else do it."

Someone Else was also among the largest givers of the church. Whenever there was a financial need, everyone just assumed that Someone Else would make up the difference.

This beloved church member was a wonderful person, sometimes appearing super-human; but a person can only do so much. Everybody expected too much of Someone Else.

Now Someone Else is gone. Who will pitch in to do the things that Someone Else has done? If you are asked to take a job in church, we hope you won't reply, "Let Someone else do it." Now we need you to pick up where Someone Else left off.

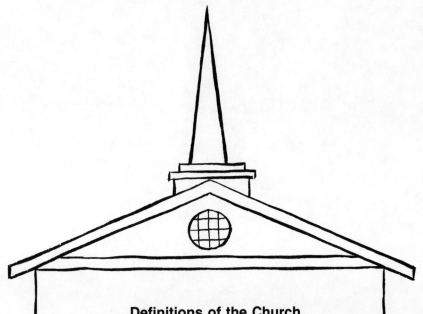

Definitions of the Church

The church is not a refrigerator for preserving perishable piety. It is a dynamo for changing human wills with power.

The church is not a store to furnish hammocks for the lazy. It is an equipping house that offers well-fitted yokes for drawing life's load.

The church is not a place to dodge life's difficulties. It is a place that furnishes strength and courage to meet them.

The Lifesaving Station:

A Modern Parable

On a dangerous seacoast where shipwrecks often happened was a makeshift lifesaving station. Its devoted workers went out day or night, searching for the lost and saving many lives. Soon the little station developed quite a reputation for its unselfish work. Many people joined the station, giving of their time, money, and effort for the support of its work. They bought new boats and trained new crews. The little lifesaving station grew.

Then, some of the new members of the station grew unhappy because the building was crude and poorly equipped. So they enlarged the building, replaced the emergency cots with comfortable beds, and put in nice furniture.

Soon the station became a popular gathering place for its members. Most of them lost interest in going to sea on lifesaving missions, so they hired a professional crew to do this work.

One day a large ship was wrecked off the coast. The hired lifesaving crew brought in boatloads of people. They were wounded, dirty, and sick. The beautiful new building was soiled and damaged. So the property committee had a shower house built outside the club where shipwreck victims could be cleaned up before coming inside.

At the next meeting, club members got into a big dispute. Most wanted to stop the lifesaving work because it interfered with their regular activities. But some members insisted that lifesaving was still their primary purpose. However, they were voted down. The majority told them if they wanted to save lives, they could start their own station down the coast. They did.

As the years passed, this new station also developed into a club, and a third lifesaving station was founded. If you visit that area today, you will find a number of exclusive clubs along the coast. Shipwrecks still happen, but most of the people drown in the stormy waters just off the shore.

—Frank G. Voight

Ten Commandments for a Happy Church

1. Speak to people. Speak to everyone, especially to those whom you don't know. There is nothing quite so nice as a cheerful word of greeting.
2. Smile at people. It takes 72 muscles to frown and only 14 to smile. Your smile is one of your finest assets. Use It! It doesn't cost a thing!!
3. Call people by name. The sweetest music to any person's ears is the sound of his or her own name. If you don't know the person's name, introduce yourself and likely the person will respond with his or her name.
4. Be friendly and helpful. If you want friends, learn to be a friend. Everyone needs them. No one has too many.
5. Be cordial. Try to speak and act as if everything you do is a genuine pleasure.
6. Be genuinely interested in people. Try to like everybody and everybody will like you. Do not limit yourself to a few friends when there are so many likable people about you.
7. Be generous with praise. And be just as sparing with criticism.
8. Be considerate of the feelings of others. Usually, there are three sides to a controversy: yours, the other person's, and the right one. Try to see them all.
9. Be alert to give service. What we do for others counts most in life. Try giving yourself away. It's fun!
10. Develop a sense of humor. To this good sense of humor, add a generous dose of patience and a dash of humility. Then get ready to receive many blessings. They're sure to come!

Prescription for Revival

If all the sleeping folk will wake up,
If all the lukewarm folk will fire up,
If all the dishonest folk will confess up,
If all the disgruntled folk will cheer up,
If all the depressed folk will cheer up,
If all the estranged folk will make up,
If all the gossipers will shut up,
If all the true soldiers will stand up,
If all the dry bones will shake up,
If all the church members will
pray up . . .

Then we can have a revival!
—R. G. Lee

The Church Is Alive and Well

In spite of what some people say and think about the church, no other institution has lasted as long.

No other organization has had a greater impact for good. From the church have sprung hospitals, nursing homes, universities, public schools, liberation movements, concepts of human dignity, child-care agencies, and the concept of democracy.

Millions of people attend athletic events every year, but many more than that attend churches and synagogues. Professional sports events gross millions, but Christians give billions to their churches as free-will gifts.

With so many negative things being said about the church, we need to pause occasionally and declare that it is still alive and well. Just think, the church is the greatest institution in history, and you and I have the privilege of being a part of it.

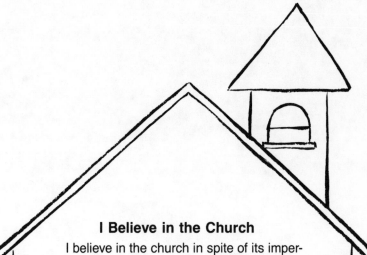

I Believe in the Church

I believe in the church in spite of its imperfections. The church will never be perfect in this world. It is made up of people struggling to do God's will—but people who are still human with their weaknesses and sin.

I believe in the church in spite of its limitations and handicaps. Sometimes the church is hindered by lack of vision and commitment. But in spite of all of this, the church is the only agency in the world that provides a place where people can gather to worship God.

I believe in the church because it is an agency of God's Spirit—an instrument of the Eternal. It has changed through the years, and it will continue to change. It will make mistakes. But the church is still God's chosen vessel for carrying on His work of redemption in the world.

Why Are Fire Trucks Red?

Fire trucks have four wheels and eight firefighters, and four plus eight equals twelve. There are twelve inches in a foot. A foot is a ruler. Queen Elizabeth is a ruler, and the *Queen Elizabeth* is one of the largest ships on the seven seas. Seas have fish. Fish have fins. The Finns fought the Russians. The Russians are red. Fire trucks are always rushin'. Therefore, fire trucks are usually red!

If you think this is wild, you ought to hear some people trying to explain why they are not attending Sunday school and church on Sunday morning!

Parable of the Dead Church

A person once called a pastor to say he wanted to join the church. But, he went on to explain that he didn't want to worship every week, study the Bible, visit the sick, witness to non-Christians, or serve as a leader or teacher.

The pastor commended him for his desire to join, but told him the church he sought was located in another section of town. The man took the directions and hung up.

When he arrived at the church, the man came face to face with the logical result of his own apathetic attitude. There stood an abandoned church building, boarded up and ready for demolition.

What I Could Do if I Really Wanted to

If I wanted to, I could help make this church the most wide awake and working church in all the world.

If I wanted to, I could show more devotion in worship and receive much more good from the services myself.

If I wanted to, I could visit members who are sick or home bound and find other ways of helping them.

If I wanted to, I could profit more from the sermon by not resenting the truth when it reveals some of my weaknesses.

If I wanted to, I could attend Bible classes regularly and encourage others to do the same.

If I wanted to, I could tell others about Christ and His church and lead them to him.

Of course, this all depends on what I want to do. I could be an honored servant of the greatest of all kings. I have the ability—if I really want to.

How to Be a Church Member without Being Religious

1. Put your name on the membership roll, but let everyone know that you don't want to get involved.
2. Be sure to take off for the lake most weekends so you can worship God in the great outdoors.
3. Do whatever gives you the most pleasure. After all, you can always ask for forgiveness later.
4. Squeal loudly when someone gets on the subject of money. Jesus never asked anyone for a donation.
5. Criticize the leaders of your congregation. They probably need someone to keep them humble.
6. Don't assume any responsibilities in the life of the church. It might cause you to spend too much time away from your family.
7. Chauffeur your children to and from Sunday school. Let God know that you are trying your best to be a Christian parent.
8. Never bring your faith into your home or business life. People might label you a religious fanatic.
9. Daydream during your pastor's sermons. You've heard all that stuff before.
10. Keep a Bible on display in your living room. It looks nice when company comes.
11. Pray if you ever get in a really big jam. This lets God know you're still around.
12. Spend Sunday mornings at home so you won't have to associate with all those hypocrites who go to church.

Six Little Ways to Mean More to Your Church

Be an On-Timer

Be a Friendly Greeter

Be a Cheerful Giver

Be a Willing Helper

Be a Hymn Singer

Be an Earnest Pray-er

The Quitter

I've taught a class for many
  years;
Borne many burdens, toiled
  through tears—
But folks don't notice me a bit,
I'm so discouraged; I'll just quit.

I've led young people day and
  night
And sacrificed to lead them right;
But folks won't help me out a
  bit—
And I'm so tired; I think I'll quit.

Christ's cause is hindered every-
  where
And people are dying in despair.
The reason why? Just think a
  bit—
The church is full of those who
  quit!

—Author unknown

Three Good Reasons to Serve Your Church

Before you say no when asked to take a job in your church, think about some reasons why you should say yes. There are at least three good reasons why every Christian ought to serve his church.

1. Your Christian life needs a service outlet. Nothing helps you to grow as a Christian like putting your faith into practice by teaching, singing, ushering, or serving on a church committee.

2. You have a testimony to share with others. The reason why you are asked to serve is that your fellow Christians have confidence in you and your ability. Your Christian testimony will be a good influence in the lives of those whom you lead and serve.

3. Your church needs you. There is no way for our church to get its work done unless members volunteer their time to teach and lead. When you accept a place of responsibility, you help your church move forward in the name of Christ.

U's Needed

You can't spell Sunday
without   U
You can't spell Church
without   U
You can't spell Budget
without   U
You can't spell Success
without   U
The church needs *U* to help.

Hitchhikers on the Church Roll

Highways aren't the only places where you'll find hitchhikers. Almost every church has plenty of members who are also looking for a free ride. They demand all the privileges and responsibilities

of church membership without supporting the congregation with their money, time, and service.

Don't be a hitchhiking Christian. Get fully involved in the life and ministry of your church. Aren't you glad Jesus wasn't looking for a free ride as he faced the decision of going to the cross on your behalf? Church membership that costs you nothing is worth exactly that.

Football Theology for Church Members

Quarterback sneak: Sunday school teachers entering the building five minutes late, trying to slip past the director without being seen.

Two-minute warning: A deacon on the front pew, taking long peeks at his watch so the preacher will be sure to notice.

Bench warmers: Inactive church members who are content to stay home and worship by watching one of the "electronic preachers" on television.

Huddle: A gathering of men outside the building for small talk and a quick smoke before the worship service begins.

"In the pocket": Where too many church members keep their tithe.

Extra point: What each member receives when he tells the preacher that the sermon was just too short!

Round Tuits Now Available for Use by Church Members

For years our church has needed a supply of *round tuits* to distribute among the membership. So we're making these available by printing a facsimile of a *round tuit* with this article. The need for this item is obvious when you hear church members make the following statements:

"I'll come to Sunday School and church just as soon as I can get around to it."

"I'll teach a class or join the choir just as soon as I can get around to it."

"I believe in tithing. I plan to do it just as soon as I can get around to it."

Be sure to clip and save this *round tuit* so you won't have any reason to say no the next time you are challenged to do something important for your church. Now that every member has his own *round tuit,* our church should really begin to move forward in the name of Christ.

The Rattlesnake Parable

Once upon a time a family that had been very active lost all interest in the church. The pastor and their fellow church members pleaded with them to get involved again, but nothing they did seemed to work.

One day the father and his sons were out in the fields working. A big rattlesnake bit one of the boys, and he became very sick. The doctor did all he could for the boy and then told the family, "All we can do now is pray." Immediately the father sent for the pastor of the church. This is the prayer the preacher is reported to have prayed:

"O wise and righteous Father, we pray for this boy's full recovery. But we also thank you for sending this rattle-snake. This family hasn't been in church for years, and we pray that this serpent will be used to bring them all to a spirit of genuine repentance. Already this snake has done more to turn them around than all the pleas of their fellow Christians. On second thought, Lord, maybe what our entire church needs are bigger and better rattlesnakes."

Who Really Broke Down Those Jericho Walls?

The pastor visited a class of boys one Sunday morning to find out what they were learning during Bible study. "Who broke down the walls of Jericho?" he asked.

"Not me, Sir," the boys replied.

"Is this typical for this class?" the pastor asked the teacher.

"These are honest boys and I believe them," the teacher replied. "I don't believe they would do a thing like that."

Frustrated and discouraged, the pastor told the Sunday school director about his visit to the class and the response of the boys and their teacher.

"Pastor, I have known the teacher and those boys for a long time," the director replied. "If they said they didn't do it, that's good enough for me."

Next, the minister brought the matter before the official board of the church. They discussed it for two hours, then reported: "Pastor, we see no need to get upset about a little thing like this. Let's just pay for any damages involved and charge it to general church maintenance."

What You Can Do for Your Pastor

Pray for him. No one needs your prayers as much as he who stands to preach the truth of God's word.

Believe in him. If he can know you believe in him with all your heart, he will be encouraged to do his best.

Stand by him. Support his visions and dreams for your church. If your church had confidence enough in his ability to call him as your leader, then stand by him.

Talk him up. Never run him down.

Give him a fair trial. All any person can ask is an honest opportunity to prove himself. Give your pastor that opportunity.

Treat him generously. Churches have often been stingy with their pastors. A little generosity will not only make his way smoother; it will also challenge him to show his appreciation by working harder.

Help him conserve time for study. Any person who speaks as often as he does must spend a great deal of time in study and prayer. Protect his time so he can devote himself to this task.

Praise him when he preaches well. He doesn't want flattery, but sincere compliments are always appreciated.

Criticize him only to his face and always in love. We can at least be men and women who meet each other openly and honestly on any matter. But more than this, we are Christians who practice love in all our relationships.

Parable of the Croaking Frogs

A farmer came to town and asked the owner of a restaurant if he could use a million frog legs. The proprietor asked where he could find so many frogs.

"I've got a pond at home just full of them," the farmer replied. "They drive me crazy night and day."

After they made an agreement for several hundred frogs, the farmer went back home. He came back a week later with two scrawny frogs and a foolish look on his face. "I guess I was wrong," he stammered. "There were just two frogs in the pond, but they sure were making a lot of noise!"

The next time you hear a lot of noise about how bad things are at church, just remember: It may be nothing more than a couple of chronic complainers who have little to do but grouch and croak!

A Teacher's Code of Ethics

As a teacher in my church, I will do my best:
To approach my task each Sunday with a prepared heart and a reverent attitude.

To make every effort to grow in the grace of the Lord Jesus Christ and to lead my pupils to do the same.

To contact absentees promptly, personally, and persistently.

To set an example in attendance, punctuality, and stewardship.

To make my instruction personal and practical, adapting the lesson to the needs of my class members.

To make a conscientious effort to win every pupil and to help him or her live as a Christian disciple.

To cooperate gladly with my pastor, Sunday school director, and other officers.

To use every possible method of improving my teaching.

To esteem Christ first, others second, and myself last.

What Music Can Do for a Child

Our church believes in providing musical training for children. As a parent you may wonder what benefits this music program can offer your children. Here are several things that music can do for children.

Music can lay foundations for Christian conversion when your child is ready for this important step.

Music can bring joy and pleasure to your child.

Music can offer your child an outlet for creative self-expression.

Music can foster a feeling of wonder, awe, and reverence in your child.

Music can help your child develop skills in group interaction and getting along with others.

Music can build your child's self-esteem by giving him an opportunity to succeed at musical presentations.

Music can provide an outlet for emotional release and satisfaction on the part of your child.

Music can supply an avenue through which your child can express his growing thoughts about God and his work in his life.

Some Advantages of Singing in the Choir

1. You never have to worry about what to wear.
2. You have excellent seats and are assured a reserved seat for Christmas and Easter.
3. From your seat in the choir loft you can gawk at, smile at, ignore, and otherwise enjoy the rest of the people in the congregation.
4. The pastor is nearly always looking the other way.
5. You're in an excellent place to see new members as they unite with the church.
6. The cost for all these benefits is low. Just one evening a week for rehearsal time.

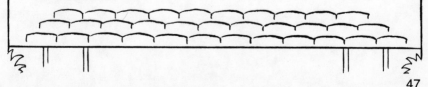

Four Excuses You'll Never Hear

"I'm staying home for several days. I don't like the way they do things at work."

"We're not going boating this afternoon. Sunday is the only day we have to rest."

"I'm not taking Joey to see a doctor. He might develop a complex about physicians."

"Forget about having the phone hooked up. We may not live here very long."

Biblical Answers to Easy Excuses

Excuse	Answer
"I'm not going to work as hard in the church this year as I did last year."	*Be thou faithful unto death, and I will give thee a crown of life* (Rev. 2:10).
"Someone else can do it better than I."	*So then every one of us shall give an account of Himself to God* (Rom. 14:12).
"I'm not qualified for the job, not educated, can't talk before people."	*My grace is sufficient for thee: for my strength is made perfect in weakness* (2 Cor. 12:9).
"I've been working too hard; I want to rest for awhile."	*If any man will come after me, let him deny himself and take up his cross daily, and follow me* (Luke 9:23).
"Someone criticized me."	*Not with eye-service, as men pleasers; but as the servants of Christ, doing the will of God from the heart; with good will doing service, as to the Lord, and not to men* (Eph. 6:6–7).
"I have so much to do when I get home from work."	*And he fell on His face, and prayed, saying, O my Father, if it be possible, let this cup pass from me: nevertheless not as I will, but as thou wilt* (Matt. 26:39).

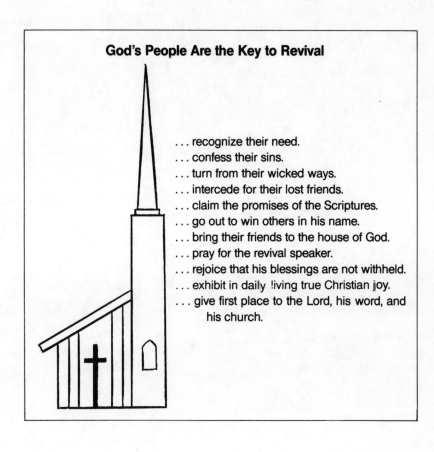

God's People Are the Key to Revival

. . . recognize their need.
. . . confess their sins.
. . . turn from their wicked ways.
. . . intercede for their lost friends.
. . . claim the promises of the Scriptures.
. . . go out to win others in his name.
. . . bring their friends to the house of God.
. . . pray for the revival speaker.
. . . rejoice that his blessings are not withheld.
. . . exhibit in daily living true Christian joy.
. . . give first place to the Lord, his word, and
      his church.

Our Call to Revival

 ecall your own Christian experience.

enew your promises to God.

esolve to do your best in his service.

 nter into the meeting wholeheartedly.

xert every effort to win someone to Christ.

nlist this person in service after his commitment.

 isualize the condition of the lost.

ow that you will do something about it.

oice your deep desire daily in prayer.

 nvite people to all the services.

mpress on them the importance of attendance.

ntensify your own efforts.

 iew the fields "white unto harvest."

olunteer your services wherever needed.

isit in homes as much as possible.

 spire to all that is good and holy.

ttend every service, if possible.

llow yourself to be used of the Lord.

 ook on the world, needy and sinful.

ove people freely, for they need your love.

et the Holy Spirit guide you.

The Mission
of Choir Members

You are the chosen of the Lord
　To sing his highest praise;
And through the medium of song
　To show his wondrous ways.

Yours is the privilege of grace;
　Your words his truth express;
Through sacred music you pro-
mote
　The cause of righteousness.

So lift your voice with one accord
　And let your anthems ring;
The people will be richly blessed,
　And God will hear you sing.
　　　　　—Author unknown

Give Us More
Pocket-Watch Christians

Many Christians are like wheelbarrows: no good unless pushed.

Others are like canoes: they need to be paddled.

Some are like kites: if you don't keep a string on them, they fly away.

Still others are like balloons: full of wind and just waiting for a chance to explode.

Then there are others like footballs: you can't tell which way they will bounce.

But praise the Lord, many Christians are like good pocket watches: with open faces and busy hands, they are well-regulated and full of good works. Christians like this are the backbone of every church.

3

Discipleship and Christian Influence

Shopping for a Cross

Jesus commanded his followers, "Take up the cross and follow me" (Mark 10:21). But too many of us want to go shopping for just the right cross rather than take up the cross of self-denial to which He referred.

Some people want a vinyl-padded cross that's not too heavy. Others look for a small, flat cross which they can put out of sight when they don't want to attract attention to the fact that they are Christians. Still others look for a jeweled cross which can make them part of the fashionable in-crowd.

But the cross of authentic Christian discipleship is a plain, rough, wooden cross that takes a lot of effort to carry. This is the type of cross on which Jesus was crucified. And this is the cross of discipleship which we as his followers must carry. But one important difference is that Jesus himself has promised to stand with us and help us bear the load. The one who directed, "Take up the cross" also declared, "My yoke is easy, and my burden is light" (Matt. 11:30).

Is Not a Passing Grade

The shepherd could have said, "I've got a pretty good record tonight. Only one sheep absent. That gives me a grade of 99 percent." But he didn't! Instead he left the security of the fold and went into the night to look for the one sheep that was lost.

A mother could say, "All is well tonight. Four of my children are safe at home and only one is lost in the darkness." But she wouldn't! Instead she would leave no stone unturned until her other child was found and safe.

A Christian can say, "I've visited and visited, but the people just won't come to my church. I think I'll stop visiting and inviting." But he won't if he remembers the example of Jesus.

Jesus' concern for each person in this world surpasses the concern of the shepherd for one lost sheep or a mother for one lost child. "God so loved the world" also means "God so loved each one in the world."

More of our members need to have the viewpoint of the Good Shepherd. He was not satisfied with a grade of 99 per cent!

Hand in Hand, a Child and I

Dear Lord, I do not ask
That thou shouldst give me some
    high work of thine,
Some noble calling or some
    wondrous task.
Give me a little hand to hold in
    mine;
Give me a little child to point the
    way
Over the strange, sweet path that
    leads to thee;
Give me a little voice to teach to
    pray;
Give me two shining eyes thy
    face to see.

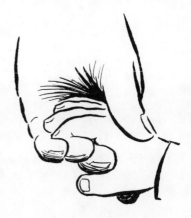

The only crown I ask, dear Lord,
    to wear is this—
That I may teach a little child.
I do not ask that I should ever
    stand among the wise
The worthy, or the great; I only
    ask that softly,
Hand in hand,
A child and I may enter at thy
    gate.

            —Author unknown

Lament of a Lost Friend

My friend, I stand in Judgment
    now
And feel that you're to blame
    somehow—
On earth I knew you day by day,
But you refused to point the way.

You taught me many things, that's
    true;
I called you friend and trusted
    you;
But I learn now that it's too late—
You could have kept me from this
    fate.

You knew the Lord in all his glory,
But you did not tell me the
    story—
And now on coming to the end,
I can no longer call you friend.
                    —Author unknown

A Matter of Perspective

Funny how $10.00 looks so big
    when you take it to
    church . . . and so small
    when you take it to the store.

Funny how laborious it is to
    read a chapter in the Bi-
    ble . . . and how easy it is to
    read a best-selling novel.

Funny how we can't think of
    anything to say when we
    pray . . . but we don't have
    any difficulty talking on the
    phone or over the back fence
    with a neighbor.

On second thought, maybe
these things aren't so funny
after all. Perhaps they reflect
our mixed-up priorities. Maybe
our problem is that we're view-
ing our commitment to God
through the wrong end of a tele-
scope.

Called Back
by the Shepherd

One bad thing about sheep is that they have a tendency to stray. They put their heads down and start grazing without watching where they are going. They have such poor sense of direction that they will graze right up to and over a cliff. So if a sheep strays, it's generally in danger. The shepherd has to go out and find it and restore it to the flock.

Aren't we often like that? We simply wander off from our Shepherd. But even though we may stray again and again, when we say, "Lord, forgive me," He brings us safely home (Ezek. 34:16).

The Bible says, "All we like sheep have gone astray; we have turned every one to his own way" (Isa. 53:6). But the Word of God also emphasizes that we can be "returned unto the Shepherd" (1 Peter 2:25)— the eternal, loving God who calls us back to fellowship with Him.

Prayer
of a Half-Hearted Christian

I love thy church, O God;
  Her walls before me stand;
But please excuse my absence, Lord;
  This bed is simply grand!

A charge to keep I have;
  A God to glorify;
But, Lord, don't ask for cash from me;
  Thy glory comes too high.

Am I a soldier of the cross,
  A follower of the Lamb?
Yes! Though I seldom pray or pay,
  I still insist I am.

Must Jesus bear the cross alone,
  And all the world go free?
No! Others, Lord, should do their part,
  But please don't count on me.

Praise God from whom all blessings flow;
  Praise him, all creatures here below!
Oh, loud my hymns of praise I bring,
  Because it doesn't cost to sing!

67

Wanted: Backbone People

What our church needs are more people with the right kinds of bones. There are at least four different types around most churches:

Wishbone People

> They hope for, they long for,
>   They wish for and sigh;
> They want things to be done
>   But aren't willing to try.

Funnybone People

> They laugh, grin, and giggle,
>   And twinkle the eye;
> If work were a joke,
>   They would give it a try.

Jawbone People

> They scold, jaw, and sputter;
>   They froth, rave, and cry;
> They're long on the talk
>   But short on the try.

Backbone People

> They strike from the shoulder,
>   They never say die;
> They're the winners in life,
>   Since they're willing to try.

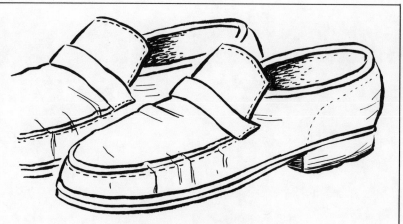

Wanted: A Pair of Shoes

Nothing fancy. Any kind will do. The main requirement is that they be motivated by a heart of love—love so strong that it causes feet to walk to a distant apartment or the house next door to tell the people who live there about the love of God.

Search your closet to see if you have a pair of shoes that might be willing to get involved in the ministry of telling others about Jesus Christ.

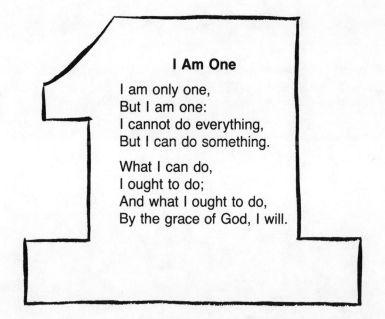

I Am One

I am only one,
But I am one:
I cannot do everything,
But I can do something.

What I can do,
I ought to do;
And what I ought to do,
By the grace of God, I will.

What Jesus Has Done for His People

He descended that we might ascend (John 6:38; John 14:3).

He became poor that we might become rich (2 Cor. 8:9; James 2:5).

He was born that we might be born again (John 1:14; John 3:2).

He became a servant that we might be sons (Phil. 2:7; Gal. 4:6, 7).

He had no home that we might have a home in heaven (Matt. 8:20; John 14:2).

He was hungry that we might be fed (Matt. 4:2; John 6:50).

He was thirsty that we might drink of the wells of salvation (John 19:28; Isa. 12:3).

He was wearied that we might rest (John 4:6; Matt. 11:29).

He was stripped that we might be clothed (Matt. 27:28; 2 Cor. 5:4).

He was forsaken that we might not be forsaken (Matt. 27:46; Heb. 13:5).

He was sad that we might be glad (Isa. 53:3; Phil. 4:4).

He was bound that we might go free (Matt. 27:2; John 8:32-36).

He was made sin that we might be made righteous (2 Cor. 5:21).

He died that we might live (John 19:33; John 5:24, 25).

He will come down that we may be caught up (1 Thess. 4:16, 17).

JESUS:

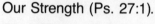

What Jesus Means to the Believer

Our Strength (Ps. 27:1).

Our Wisdom (1 Cor. 1:30).

Our Sanctification (1 Cor. 1:30).

Our Righteousness (2 Cor. 5:21).

Our Redemption (1 Cor. 1:30).

Our Peace (John 16:33; Eph. 2:14).

Our Victory (1 Cor. 15:57; Col. 2:15).

Our Joy (John 15:11).

Our Hope (Col. 1:27).

Our Obedience (Heb. 10:7).

Our Spiritual Fullness (Col. 2:9-10).

Our Goodness (Gal. 5:22).

Our Source of Love (John 17:26; 1 John 4:8).

Our Kindness (Gal. 5:22).

Our Source of Forgiveness (Luke 23:34).

Our Patience (Gal. 5:22).

Our Rest (Matt. 11:28; Heb. 4:10).

Our Self-Control (Gal. 5:23).

Our Freedom (Col. 2:16-17).

Our Gentleness (Gal. 5:22).

Our Spiritual Mind (1 Cor. 2:16).

Our Faithfulness (Gal. 5:22).

Our Access to God (John 14:6; Eph. 3:21).

Our LIFE (Phil. 1:21; Col. 3:4).

A Moment with Him

We mutter and sputter
  We fume and we spurt,
We mumble and grumble,
  Our feelings get hurt.

We can't understand things,
  Our vision grows dim,
When all that we need
  Is a moment with HIM.

—Author unknown

Make Me a Rain

I am only a spark; make me a fire.
I am only a string; make me a lyre.
I am only a drop; make me a fountain.
I am only an ant hill; make me a mountain.
I am only a feather; make me a wing.
I am only a serf; make me a king.
I am only a link; make me a chain.
I am only a sprinkle; make me a rain.

—Author unknown

The Story of Everybody,
Somebody, Anybody, and Nobody

Once upon a time there were four men named Everybody, Somebody, Anybody, and Nobody. There was an important job to be done and Everybody was asked to do it. But Everybody was sure that Somebody would do it. Anybody could have done it. But Nobody did it. Somebody got angry about it, because it was Everybody's job. Everybody thought that Anybody could do it, and Nobody realized that Everybody wouldn't do it. It ended up that Everybody blamed Somebody and Nobody did the job that Anybody could have done in the first place. At last report, these four men were still arguing and the job they were supposed to do still wasn't done.

Sentence Sermon

Watch Your Roads

Just because it's a well-beaten road is no sign it's the right one.

Sentence Sermon

Maturity Defined

You have become a mature person when keeping a secret gives you more satisfaction than passing it along.

Sentence Sermon

Never Too Old

It's funny how you never get too old to learn some new ways to be foolish.

Sentence Sermon

Don't Block the Track

Even if you are on the right track, you'll get run over if you just sit there.

4

Stewardship

The Message of Money

Dug from the mountainside,
  Washed in the glen.
Servant am I
  Or master of men.

Steal me, I curse you;
  Earn me, I bless you.
Grasp me and hoard me,
  A fiend shall possess you.

Lie for me, die for me,
  Covet or take me—
Angel or devil,
  I am what you make me.
      —Author unknown

Parable of the Growing Income

A man knelt with his pastor and asked for God's blessings as he committed himself to tithe. His income that first week was $100.00, and his tithe was $10.00. As the years passed, he became more and more prosperous, until his tithe reached the level of $500.00 per week. Alarmed at the rising amount, he sought out his pastor and asked what he could do about the problem.

"When I made the promise, I only had to give ten dollars," he explained, "but now it's $500.00. I just can't afford to give away money like that."

"I can see that you really do have a problem," the pastor replied. "Maybe we can kneel right here and ask God to shrink your income so you can go back to giving ten dollars a week again."

What a Horrible Dream!

I dreamed that the Lord took my weekly contribution to the church, multiplied it by ten, and turned this amount into my weekly income. In no time I lost all my furniture, and had to give up my automobile. Why, I couldn't even make a house payment. What can a person do on $10.00 a week?

Suppose the Lord took your offering and multiplied it by ten and made that your weekly income. How much would you earn? This question might give you some fresh insights into the stewardship needs of our church.

A Sobering Stewardship Question

Ten thousand for my brand new car,
   Twelve thousand for a piece of sod,
Fifteen thousand to begin a house,
   A dollar I gave to God.

A tidy sum to entertain,
   My friends in pointless chatter,
And when the world goes crazy mad,
   I ask, "Lord, what's the matter?"

Yet, there is one big question,
   For the answer I still search,
"With things so bad in this old world,
   What's holding back the church?"

5

Seasonal and Christian Year

Promises for the New Year

This year make some promises rather than resolutions for the new year. The following list should get you started:

Promise to be so strong that nothing can disturb your peace of mind.

Promise to make all your friends feel that there is something special about them.

Promise to look at the sunny side of everything, and make your optimism come true.

Promise to think only of the best, to work only for the best, and to make the best come true.

Promise to be just as enthusiastic about the success of others as you are about your own.

Promise to forget the mistakes of the past and press on to the greater achievements of the future.

Promise to wear a cheerful expression at all times and give every person you meet a smile.

Promise to give so much effort to the improvement of yourself that you have no time to criticize others.

Promise to be too large for worry, too noble for anger, too strong for fear, and too happy to permit the presence of trouble in your life.

Prayer for the New Year

Slow Me Down, Lord,

Lord, this year teach me the art of taking minute vacations—of slowing down to look at a flower, to chat with a friend, to pat a dog, to read from the Bible.

Remind me each day that the race is not always to the swift; that there is more to life than increasing its speed. Let me look upward into the branches of the towering oak and know that it grew slowly and well.

Slow me down, Lord, and inspire me to send my roots deep into the soil of eternal values, that I may grow toward my eternal home.

Through Jesus Christ our Lord. Amen.

God's Love

For God so loved the world,
that he gave his only begotten Son,
that whosoever believeth in him
should not perish,
but have everlasting life.
—John 3:16

What to Give Up for Lent

Give up watching television one evening a week. Visit some lonely or sick person instead.

Give up looking at other people's worst points. Concentrate on their strong points and positive attributes.

Give up speaking unkindly. Let your speech be generous and understanding.

Give up your worries. Trust God with your problems and frustrations.

Give up hatred or dislike of anyone. Learn to love instead.

Give up the fear which prevents Christian witness. Seek courage to speak about your faith to others.

Give up spending so much time with newspapers and magazines. Use some of that time to study your Bible.

Give up grumbling. Learn to give thanks in everything.

Give up ten to fifteen minutes each day. Use that time in prayer.

Give up buying anything but essentials for yourself. Give that money to God's work or someone in need.

Give up judging by appearance and by the standards of the world. Learn to give up yourself to God.

Surely he hath borne our griefs, and carried our sorrows: yet we did esteem him stricken, smitten of God and afflicted. But he was wounded for our transgressions, he was bruised for our iniquities: the chastisement of our peace was upon him; and with his stripes we are healed. All we like sheep have gone astray; we have turned every one to his own way; and the Lord hath laid on him the iniquity of us all.

—Isaiah 53:4–6

The Wonder of The Empty Tomb

The ancient world boasted of seven wonders: the pyramids of Egypt; the hanging gardens of Babylon; the temple of the goddess Diana at Ephesus; the lighthouse at Alexandria, Egypt; the Colossus (huge bronze statue) in the harbor at Rhodes; the statue of the pagan god Zeus at Olympia, Greece; and the tomb of the Persian king Halicarnassus.

Of all those ancient wonders, only the pyramids are still standing. All the others have crumbled, along with the ancient world powers whose accomplishments they memorialized. But another wonder from the ancient world is still very much alive today. This wonder is more significant than all seven of these ancient landmarks put together. This is the wonder of the empty tomb of Jesus at Jerusalem.

When the body of Jesus was placed in the tomb, the forces of evil were certain they had won the victory at last. But Jesus was raised on the third day. His resurrection proved that he was more powerful than sin and death and all the other negative forces that Satan uses against us.

Wonder of wonders, Jesus lives! And his dynamic power is available to all who place their faith and trust in him.

The Legend of the Dogwood

According to legend, the dogwood tree once grew straight and tall. But then it was used to make the cross on which Jesus was crucified. As a memorial of this event, the tree never again grew large enough to be used for this purpose.

In the spring, when the dogwood blooms, the four-petal arrangement of its flowers reminds us of the cross. Each white petal has an indention on its outer edge—a symbol of the nail marks in our Savior's hands. Then, in the fall, the leaves of the dogwood turn a fiery red to commemorate the blood of Jesus with which our salvation was secured.

Portrait of a Mother

A mother can be almost any size or age, but she won't admit to anything over thirty. She has soft hands and smells good. A mother likes new dresses, music, a clean house, her children's kisses, an automatic washer, and Daddy.

A mother doesn't like having her children sick, muddy feet, temper tantrums, loud noise, or bad report cards. She can read a thermometer (much to the amazement of Daddy) and like magic, can kiss a hurt away. She can also bake good cakes and pies, but likes to see her children eat vegetables.

A mother can stuff a fat baby into a snowsuit in seconds and can kiss little faces and make them smile. She is underpaid, has long hours, and gets very little rest. She worries too much about her children. And no matter how old they are, she still likes to think of them as her little babies.

A mother is the guardian angel of the family, the queen, the tender hand of love. She is the best friend anyone ever has.

A mother is love.

—Author unknown

A Father's ABC's

A lways trust your children to God's care.

B ring them to church.

C hallenge them to high goals.

D elight in their achievements.

E xalt the Lord in their presence.

F rown on evil.

G ive them love.

H ear their problems.

I gnore not their childish fears.

J oyfully accept their apologies.

K eep their confidence.

L ive a good example before them.

M ake them your friends.

N ever ignore their endless questions.

O pen your heart to their love.

P ray for them by name.

Q uicken your interest in their spirituality.

R emember their needs.

S how them the way of salvation.

T each them to work.

U nderstand they are still young.

V erify your statements.

W ean them from bad company.

E **X** pect them to obey.

Y earn for God's best for them.

Z ealously guide them in Bible truth.

Formula for
a Strong Nation

I know three things must
    always be
To keep a nation strong and
    free.
One is a hearthstone bright
    and dear,
With busy, happy loved ones
    near.

One is a ready heart and
    hand
To love, and serve, and keep
    the land.
One is a worn and beaten way
To where the people go to
    pray.

So long as these are kept
    alive,
Nation and people will survive.
God, keep them always,
    everywhere—
The home, the heart, the
    place of prayer.

—Author unknown

Thank You, Lord

Just this once, Lord, I want to come to you with no problems, but simply to say, Thank You:

For your forgiveness when I fail

For the sheer joy of sleep when I'm terribly tired

For the silent strength of humility when pride overtakes me

For the justice of your laws when men are cruel

For the rememdies for sickness when I am ill

For the simplicity of orderliness when I face confusion

For the assurance that you have made a place especially for me when I feel inadequate among my peers

For the joy of helping others when I see people in need

For the earthly evidences of your will when I'm trying to find out what life is all about

For the reality of your world, when I stray too far into fantasy

For the rightness of reasonableness when I panic too quickly

For the fun that refreshes when everything gets too serious

For the renewal in moments of silence when I'm dizzy being busy in a hectic world.

Thank you, Lord, for all these things. But most of all, thank you for your abiding presence that makes every day I live a day of thanks.

Our Christmas Prayer

God grant you peace at
   Christmas
   And fill your heart with
   cheer;
God grant you health and
   happiness
   Throughout the coming year.
God guide you with his
   wisdom
   And keep you in his care;
This is our special wish for
   you—
   This is our Christmas prayer.
                —Author unknown

The Christmas Heart

The Christmas heart is a
   gentle heart;
Malice and envy have no part.
Coldness and bitterness
   cannot stay
Where the spirit of Christmas
   holds full sway.
Joy will enter and grief depart
When Christmas candles light
   the heart.

                —Author unknown

I
love
a star,
a wreath,
a shopping
list, a crowd,
a gift, a time
of worship, a toy,
a child, a colored
ball, a party, a kiss,
a family together, the
sound of laughter, turkey
'n mince pie, joy and peace,
a tree of lights, the glow of
candles, the faith of a child,
the sound of bells, an angel's song—
a world
at peace,
full of
love and
goodwill
for all
mankind.

Christmas Joy

Somehow, not only for
  Christmas,
  But all the long year
  through,
The joy that you give to others
  Is the joy that comes back
  to you;

And the more you spend in
  blessing
  The poor and lonely ·and
  sad,
The more of your heart's
  possessing
  Returns to make you glad.
            —John Greenleaf Whittier

What to Do
This Christmas

Mend a quarrel.

Seek out a forgotten friend.

Share some treasure.

Give a soft answer.

Encourage youth.

Keep a promise.

Find the time.

Listen.

Apologize if you were wrong.

Be gentle.

Laugh a little.

Laugh a little more.

Express your gratitude.

Welcome a stranger.

Gladden the heart of a child.

Take pleasure in the beauty
  and wonder of the earth.

Speak your love.

Speak it again.

Christic in Christmas

CHRIST, the only begotten Son of God, looked at the sinful world and realized its need for

HELP. In council with the Father it was agreed that he would give up his high and exalted place and bring to sinful men

REDEMPTION. He would go to earth in person and through the miracle of birth would become the

INCARNATION of God in human flesh. He would be born of a virgin with God as his Father, and enter into the sinful world as its

SAVIOR. His holiness, his exemplary life, his sinlessness, his plan of redemption, his death, and his resurrection would bring to earth the great

TRANSFORMATION needed by all mankind. So he came, as decided in the councils of eternity, and through his coming he brought the

MELODY of heaven to earth. A babe in swaddling clothes, divine, whose birth was announced by the singing of angels on high was to bring

ASSURANCE to all mankind that God cared enough to send his only begotten Son that all who believe in him might have

SALVATION and eternal life. Only through personal acceptance of him, God's great gift to man, can there be real Christmas in the human heart.